2 079677 21

D0783789

741·9492

BONNIER

RESERVE

14. DEC. 1982

741.9492

Bonnier: ✗

RENFREW DISTRICT LIBRARIES

SED

....Branch

NOT TO BE W/D
SUC

This book is to be returned on or before
the last date above. It may be borrowed
for a further period if not in demand.

JAN '84

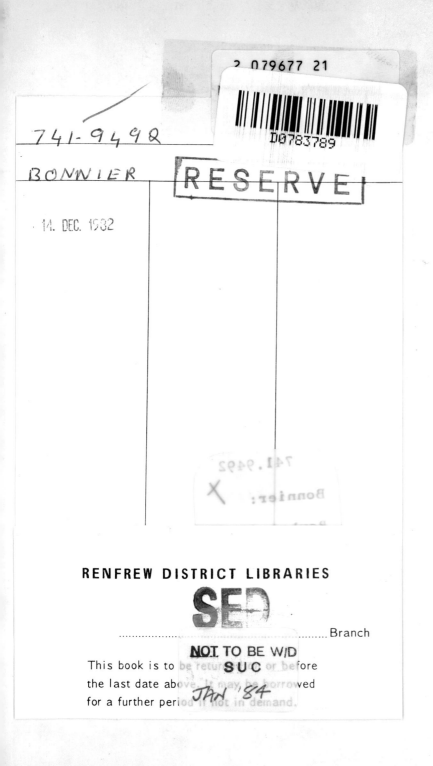

The Great Draughtsmen

Rembrandt

Rembrandt
Translated by Victoria Benedict

General Editor
Henri Scrépel
Originally published in French under the title
l'Univers de Rembrandt, *in the series* Les Carnets de Dessins.
Copyright © 1968 by Henri Scrépel, Paris.

The author wishes to acknowledge his debt
to Claude Roger-Marx in *Rembrandt* (Charles Tisné, 1960),
to Charles Wilson in *The Dutch Republic* (McGraw-Hill, 1969),
and to Otto Benesch in *Rembrandt* (Skira, n.d.)

Pall Mall Press Ltd.,
5 Cromwell Place, London SW7

First published in Great Britain in 1970.
All rights reserved.

ISBN 0 269 02711 4
Printed in France.

Rembrandt

Henry Bonnier

RENFREW COUNTY LIBRARY

Pall Mall Press London

Rembrant

741.9492
Bonnier
1

1. The Holy Family in Joseph's Workshop, about 1640-42
Pen and wash with bistre and India ink

Louvre, Paris

2079677 21
A. 13.7.70.

Contents

2.
Self-portrait, about 1627-28
Pen and bistre, brush and
India ink

British Museum, London

The Enigma of Rembrandt

Last year commemorated the third centenary of Rembrandt's death, which occured on October 4, 1669. For three hundred years the greatest minds have examined both the artist and his work without solving the enigma he represents.

Marivaux, who was an excellent judge of human nature, suggested that the soul can be glimpsed, *"pour ainsi dire, au visage"* ("in the face"), and Lavater wrote a treatise on *l'art de connaître les hommes par la physionomie* (The Art of Knowing Man by His Physiognomy). Rembrandt, in fact, left more self-portraits than any other painter: sixty-two paintings catalogued by Bredius, sixteen drawings certified by Otto Benesch, and twenty-eight etchings authenticated by Ludwig Münz—more than one hundred self-portraits in all, made between 1626, when he was twenty years old, and 1669, the year of this death. But, with all due respect to Marivaux and Lavater, this superabundance of self-portraits only deepens the mystery of Rembrandt for me. How did Rembrandt conceive of his inextricably linked life and work, to have been attracted to the point of fascination by his own image? Each one of the self-portraits betrays the persistent, painful, passionate interrogation of a man in search of himself. Questioned, questioning, imprisoned by his own quest, the painter ultimately refers us to the initial enigma of the man himself.

3. The Reading, about 1631   Pen and brush, washes in gray   Bonnat Museum, Bayonne

I

The Environment

When Charles V of Germany abdicated in 1555, because of ill health, he left the hereditary states of Austria and the imperial crown to his brother Ferdinand, and Spain, Italy, the New World, and the Netherlands to his son Philip.

The Dutch provinces which fell to Spain covered an area approximately equivalent to that of the present Benelux countries, stretching from Friesland in the north to the French border in the south, and from the shores of the North Sea in the west to the frontiers of Germany in the east. They undoubtedly constituted the most heavily populated, most active, and richest Germanic part of the Holy Roman Empire, and the populace was profoundly disturbed by the abdication of Charles V, a native of Ghent.

However, this bond did not prevent rebellion against the Spanish, which was provisionally halted in 1609 with a truce that sanctioned the separation of Spain and the United Provinces and gave new life to the Dutch Republic which, formed by the Treaty of Utrecht in 1581, consisted solely of the northern provinces. Only in 1648 did the Treaty of Munster's formal recognition of the Republic's independence finally put an end to the Thirty Years' War. What explanation is there for the strife that ravaged the Netherlands for eighty years after Charles's abdication (with the exception of the Twelve Years' Truce)? What motivated the Dutch to rise against Spain, and why did only the seven northern provinces succeed in winning their independence?

The world into which Rembrandt was born in 1606 and the environment in which the child, and then the man, lived are better understood in relationship to the interdependent political, economic, geographical, and religious conditions responsible for the independent movement. *"L'œil écoute"* ("the eye listens"), Paul Claudel justly remarked in explaining why, before listening to Rembrandt—since every work of art is a silence to be heard—we should hark to the clamor that preceded his birth and shaped the mentality of his contemporaries: the yellow clash of arms, of course; but also the red cries of stevedores in the port of Amsterdam; and the violet laughter of its life-loving citizenry; the green and blue activity of men and merchandise; the preachers' ochre exhortations; and the black and white words of the syndics and professors.

An artist's palette contains a flurry of shouts and groans, laughter and tears; Rembrandt's palette contained everyday Holland, its essential truths renewed, deepened, and more beloved from year to year, to the point of such total identification that Rembrandt himself, in his own way, came to express Holland.

4. The Lamentation, about 1659-60
Pen and wash

Graphische Sammlung, Munich

5. Head of an Oriental in a Turban,
with a Dead Bird of Paradise, about 1637
Pen and wash in bistre, white gouache

Louvre, Paris

6. The Baptism of the Eunuch, about 1629 .   Black chalk   Graphische Sammlung, Munich

7. Saskia Carrying Rumbartus
Downstairs, about 1636
Pen and wash in bistre

Pierpont Morgan Library, New York

8.
Two Studies of a
Bird of Paradise,
about 1637

Pen and bistre,
some washes,
white gouache

Louvre, Paris

The Dutch Resistance

The modern conviction that nothing can restrain a nation bent on obtaining its independence is a political simplification of the complexities of such movements. More accurate is Charles Wilson's explanation in *The Dutch Republic:* "it was not a single movement; it was a *congeries* of revolts...." The explosion was ignited by Philip II's frustrating confrontation with medieval structures, when he tried to strengthen his power by imposing on his Dutch possessions political modernizations similar to those in France, England, and Spain. Wilson explains; "Nowhere was the overmighty subject so unbiddable, the burgher richer or more obstinate, nor the prince more hard up." This was so true that the rebellion could have lasted indefinitely had not the nobility, led by William of Nassau, succeeded in winning over the middle-class merchants. Infuriated to see his governmental reforms foundering in a morass of established privileges and traditional liberties in spite of his decision to suppress the rebel provinces, Philip II tried "to crush ... their essential national laws, their privileges, and former rights" (Sir Walter Raleigh, cited by Wilson).

The almost immediate result was the birth of a nation—an unusual nation which had, in fact, existed long before the rebellion against Spain and was formed, not by the common history of its people, but by their incessant fight to conquer a most uncommon land.

"La Hollande n'est qu'un tas de boue au milieu des eaux" ("Holland is just a mud cake surrounded by water") wrote Taine, with the afterthought, *"Joignez à cette inclémence du sol la rigueur de la température, et vous serez tentés de conclure que le pays n'est pas fait pour l'homme, mais pour les échassiers et les castors"* ("Add the severity of the temperature to the inclemency of the soil, and you will be tempted to conclude that the country was not destined for man, but for the stiltbird and the beaver"). This statement is illustrated by the manner in which the country has been molded by human hands, every inch redeemed from the sea by dikes and canals.

The land of Holland, "low land" *("pays creux")*, "earthy land" *("terre charnelle")*, as Peguy would have said, gave birth to a spirit that was stronger than elsewhere because the land demanded constant reconquest, unceasing proof of possession and worthiness over the sea and above all over oneself. Without the Dutch there could have been no Holland. The Rustringen oath which rings like a proclamation: "We will fight in ebb and flow; we will battle day and night with spade and pitchfork, as long as the wind blows," and a Zealand proverb: "He who is unable to fend off the waters does not deserve the land," reveal the elements necessary for the formation of a very special kind of character.

The Land of Holland

The land consists of a thin straight skyline that alternates between the green of the pastures and the red of brick houses under the weight of an immense, endless sky. And to all appearances, the Dutchman balances like an acrobat on land whose very existence is miraculous. The admirably well-found national motto, *Luctor et emergo* ("I fight and I emerge") suggests that, if the fight is relinquished, the land will be invaded and reduced to a quagmire before eventually disappearing, whereas resistance can obtain freedom from the mud, an emergence in the biological sense of the word: "the appearance of new properties in the course of development or evolution that could not have been foreseen in an earlier stage." To maintain the equilibrium between foundering and emergence demanded a constant personal struggle as well as a fight against the elements—a need to dominate oneself, to surpass oneself, and to be perpetually wary.

In his struggle, the Dutchman appears to teeter, at the limit of the material, on the skyline that separates sky from sea—that unfriendly and at the same time motherly sea against which all energies must be mustered and, yet, from which come great riches. Pliny the Elder had already remarked of this country that "one is unable to say if it belongs more to the sea or to the land." In view of the extraordinary works it has produced, I should reply that it belongs neither to the sea nor to the land, but to its eternally changing sky.

Their relentless struggle quickly distinguished the Dutch from the inhabitants of the southern provinces, and this difference of character probably explains, at least in part, the north's conversion to Calvinism while Flanders remained Catholic. In any event, we know that the new republic included only the northern provinces ruled by the Calvinists, whereas by 1579 the overwhelmingly Catholic southern provinces had given up the fight against Spain in exchange for military and political concessions.

A geographical element must be added to the religious and economic incentives for independence. As their name indicates, the northern provinces were located north of a barrier formed first by the Meuse and Rhine Rivers and then by two branches of the Rhine, the Waal and the Lek, and deepened by the large estuaries of these rivers. By entrenching itself behind this natural defense, the Netherlands created a geographical delimitation to the Calvinist resistance. Once again religion was to precede and outline the political action that followed.

9. Dying Boy, about 1636   Pen and wash in bistre   Louvre, Paris

     Dutch independence was marked by two characteristics that reappear constantly in Rembrandt's Holland. First, there was a false but admittedly original nationalism due more to geographical than to historical conditions and more to a daily awareness than to a conscious theory. Secondly, Calvinism provided an ideological crutch rather than a motive for the wars. Here again the situation in the Netherlands was novel since the Reformation probably owed its success there to the fertile ground provided by the mercantile society which it opportunely justified by relating profit with merit. In short, the religious, historical, and political aspects of the Dutch independence movement were basically shaped by commercial considerations subject, in turn, to certain geographical conditions.

10. Rumbartus on his Deathbed, about 1638
    Pen and bistre, wash

    Rijksmuseum, Amsterdam

11. Women in a Doorway,
    about 1635
Brush, pen and wash

Private collection

Orbi ex Orbe

"Subsister, s'abriter, se vêtir, manger, se pourvoir contre le froid et l'humidité, s'approvisionner, s'enrichir, ils n'avaient point le temps de penser à autre chose" ("They had time only to subsist, find shelter, clothing, and nourishment, to provide against the cold and damp, to stock the larder, and to prosper"), wrote Taine of the Dutch; and they were, in fact, to transform their country into a vast storage depot. No words better express the mercantile character of the Dutch than the motto of Rotterdam, *Orbi ex orbe* ("We return to the world what the world gives us")—an ambiguous concept which implies that Holland originated nothing, for the Dutch proved their merit as international intermediaries by developing a talent for transforming and reselling what they received from all parts of the world. As we shall see, the motto of Rotterdam also applied to Rembrandt in his appropriation and adaptation of the styles of foreign artists.

The proud, stern motto was dictated by trade and left little room for revery, but, for the moment the Dutch had neither the time nor the inclination to dream. Holland was experiencing a period of intense prosperity, due apparently to the war against Spain, which advantageously increased the Dutch population with Protestants from the southern provinces and a large colony of Spanish and Portuguese Jews, and brought about a naval innovation which was to make Holland the mistress of maritime transportation. The *fluit*, an inexpensive, flat-bottomed freighter whose Dutch name was derived from the French *flûte*, or *flibot*, appeared on the high seas about 1590 and enabled the United Provinces to create an enormous colonial empire.

In 1602 came the founding of the East India Company, probably one of the first joint stock companies ever to exist. This kind of state-within-a-state owned trading posts in the Moluccas and in Persia, founded the town of Batavia in Java, and eventually controlled all trade with China and India. At the same time a West India Company was created, under whose auspices Henry Hudson founded New Amsterdam.

After the Truce of 1609, a Discount Bank was established in Amsterdam to organize and regulate these different activities. This completely unoriginal bank was based on an Italian model, the Bank of Venice, and represented yet another incarnation of the Rotterdam motto. From the time of the bank's inception, the United Provinces relayed *La Serenissima* (the Most Serene Republic) in money matters, adopting not only the Venetian banking system but also its methods of marine insurance and of double-entry accounting. The Netherlands made no original contribution of its own in this field until Hugo Grotius laid the foundations of modern international law.

12. The Baptism of the Eunuch, about 1655   Reed pen and wash in bistre   Graphische Sammlung, Munich

13. The Good Samaritan at the Door of the Inn, about 1640-42
    Pen and wash in bistre

    Louvre, Paris

14. The Entombment of Christ,
about 1640-41
Pen and wash in bistre

Kupferstichkabinett, Dresden

Pragmatism and Liberalism

The Dutch believed in a law of precedent that contrasted sharply with the judicial formalism of the Latins. Their commercial success in the first part of the seventeenth century amply proves the degree to which this attitude stimulated the spirit of enterprise.

Pragmatism necessarily entails liberalism, and both these concepts, which were formed by commercial considerations, influenced the religious behavior of the Dutch. One must remember that commercial liberalism encouraged Calvin's doctrines and not the other way around. This peculiar combination of elements explains clearly, I think, how, at the height of its prosperity, Holland was able to avoid a theocratic form of government in spite of the wishes of most of its preachers. Nevertheless, Calvin's strong religion was well suited to this primitive people, who were trained to venture across the seas in their quest for spices.

This type of liberalism gave Amsterdam an air of eccentricity in the midst of totalitarian Europe. The fact that in 1622 immigrants from the southern provinces and their descendants were thought to comprise one-third of the city's population (Wilson) qualified Holland as an exchange society for men as well as for goods. In about 1640, Andrew Marvell, surprised and sarcastic, described in his long poem, *The Character of Holland:*

> Hence Amsterdam, Turk-Christian-Pagan-Jew,
> Staple of Sects and Mint of Schisme grew;
> That Bank of Conscience, where not one so strange,
> Opinion but finds Credit, and Exchange.

On the other hand, Spinoza held up his native city as an example: "Take the city of Amsterdam, whose enjoyment of this freedom has made it great and admired by the whole world. In this flourishing state, this city without a peer, men of every race and sect live in the greatest harmony ... " *(Tractatus Theologico-Politicus).* In a letter dated May 5, 1631 and addressed to his friend Jean-Louis Guez de Balzac, Descartes also extolled Amsterdam in terms made all the more interesting by their revelation of the discomforts that awaited the traveler or philosopher elsewhere: "*En cette grande ville où je suis, n'y ayant aucun homme excepté moi, qui n'exerce la marchandise, chacun y est tellement attentif à son profit, que j'y pourrais demeurer toute ma vie sans y être jamais vu de personne.... Quel autre lieu pourrait-on choisir au reste du monde où toutes les commodités de la vie, et toutes les curiosités qui peuvent être souhaitées, soient si faciles à trouver qu'en celui-ci? Quel autre pays où l'on puisse jouir d'une liberté aussi entière, où l'on puisse dormir avec moins d'inquiétude, où il*

15. Thatched Cottages with a Cart in Front, about 1640-41
Pen and wash in bistre

Louvre, Paris

y ait toujours des armées sur pied exprès pour nous garder, où les empoisonnements, les trahisons, les calomnies soient moins connues?" ("Everyone is so concerned with his own business in this big city, in which I alone am not a tradesman, that I could remain here all my life without being noticed.... Where else in the world are all of life's necessities and every imaginable curiosity so easily available? Where else can one enjoy such complete freedom and sleep so peacefully as here, guarded by armed forces ever ready to defend us in a country where poisoning, treachery, and slander are almost unknown?") (*Correspondance*, ed. Adam and Tannery, I, 203, 204).

Freedom

The word constantly reappears in the writing of Spinoza, Descartes, Marvell, and others. After the Truce of Antwerp, the United Provinces undoubtedly became a kind of political, economic, and religious phenomena, even an anomaly. The craze to invest, to make money, and to speculate that possessed Holland during the first half of the seventeenth century is understandable when one remembers that this small country was on the verge of attaining the status of a great power, after it had succeeded in gaining a colonial empire obviously well beyond its means. The extraordinary proliferation of painters in Holland at this time was born directly of the commercial situation. Each newly enriched middle-class family wanted to be realistically represented at home—and one does enter a painting of this period as one would an interior. Every household wanted to have its own paintings, which were considered investments. The philosopher Jean-Toussaint Desanti perhaps explained, in part, the flourishing of art when he wrote in his *Introduction à l'Histoire de la Philosophie*, " *La pratique du grand commerce développe la connaissance de la nature*" ("Big business develops a knowledge of nature"). However, it would be a mistake to think of the golden age of Dutch painting as a profitable period for the artists.

The large middle-class clientele was stingy and considered painting utilitarian. The fact that *schoon*, the Dutch word for "beautiful," soon came to mean "clean," gives a good indication of the seventeenth-century attitude. Since, under the Republic living conditions remained more or less the same as before, Antwerp continued to claim as many painters as butchers or bakers (Wilson). The great majority of these artists lived in extreme poverty. To mention only the most famous: Hals, Hobbema, and Ruysdaël died in the poorhouse; Hercules Seghers became an alcoholic; Van Laar committed suicide; Vermeer died heavily in debt to his baker.

Under these circumstances, how can one explain the simultaneous birth of so many different talents in Holland when, during the same period, other European countries produced only one painter around whom the nation's art was oriented? Caravaggio in Italy, Poussin in France, Rubens in Flanders, Velazquez in Spain. ... In addition to the social, economic, and philosophic reasons already discussed, this question calls

16. View of London, with Old St. Paul's, about 1640
Pen and bistre, wash, white gouache

Kupferstichkabinett, Berlin

for a religious answer, which explains the true originality of the period. By rejecting any kind of decoration or painting in the churches, Calvinist iconoclasm secularized Dutch art at a time when everywhere else religious art, in Raymond Cogniat's words, *"sous la poussée du courant baroque, s'épanouissait et s'enrichissait d'un évident paganisme"* ("blossomed and thrived on obvious paganism, under the influence of the Baroque movement") *(La Peinture du XVIIe Siècle).*

17. The Conspiracy of Julius Civilis, about 1660-61
Pen and bistre

Graphische Sammlung, Munich

This brief survey provides only a few guidelines, since the nature of our book calls for brevity. Many points merit elaboration: outstanding moments of the rebellion (for example, *"Les Gueux de mer"*); the idea of freedom that Julius Civilis taught the Batavian ancestors of the Dutch; the advantage taken by Amsterdam of the discovery of a new route to India that bore a mortal blow to the Republic of Venice; and the way in which the sixteenth century foreshadowed, prepared, and provoked the fulfillments of the seventeenth century. But even then our history would remain incomplete until the name Erasmus was mentioned.

It is difficult to seize the quintessence or the mentality of a nation at a given time. And yet, this is essentially what we are trying to do: to put ourselves in the place of Rembrandt's contemporaries, to feel their mood and know their customs so that this giant of painting appears more vividly as the people of Amsterdam saw, valued, and then condemned him; and also, as he came to know the labyrinths within himself, like the mole who grandly answered an inquiry as to the meaning of its underground burrowing and obscure wanderings: "I divine myself."

18. Thatched Cottages in Sunlight under a Stormy Sky, about 1641
Pen, washes in bistre and India ink

Albertina, Vienna

19. Three Thatched Cottages, about 1640-41
Pen and bistre, wash, some white gouache

National Museum, Stockholm

II

Rembrandt

Born in Leiden on July 15, 1606, Rembrandt Harmensz (son of Armand) was the sixth son of a Leiden miller, Harmen Gerritsz, and the daughter of a local baker. Thus, by birth he belonged to the well-to-do lower middle class; in his will, the father listed his possessions as a town house located on the Weddesteegh, a draff mill on Pelican Wharf (draff is the dregs of ground, germinated barley used in brewing beer), and other houses in Leiden proper. Because the mill was situated on the bank of the Rhine, his father added "van Rijn" to his signature, a surname adopted by Rembrandt after *R.H.* (Rembrandt Harmensz), *R.L.* (Rembrandt van Leiden), and *R.H.L.* (Rembrandt Harmensz van Leiden).

Although almost nothing is known of Rembrandt's early childhood except that he attended the *"petite école,"* a kind of kindergarten and elementary school, it is not difficult to imagine the life led by Dutch children at this time. In good weather, a child too young for school spent the better part of the day playing in the street, so that he would not dirty the house, if his family were wealthy, or for lack of space, if the family were poor. In *Daily Life in Rembrandt's Holland*, Paul Zumthor writes, "So the Dutch town swarmed from morning onwards with children from three to six years old, of all classes of society, mixed into a playing, yelling, fighting mass on the pavements, under the house canopies, along the streets." I leave it to the reader to judge the surprise and bewilderment of foreign visitors before such methods of bringing up children, which certainly did not encourage discipline, even though the children had to respect certain manners and to address their parents as "Sir my father" and "Madam my mother."

Parental authority was so weak that in 1641 in his *Beschrijving der Stad Leiden* (Description of Leiden) the burgomaster, Johannes Orlers, described the already famous Rembrandt as follows: "His parents sent him to school to learn Latin in view of attending and graduating from the Leiden Academy, an education which would have prepared the young man to serve his town and community; but he showed absolutely no inclination for his studies since he was instinctively interested only in painting and drawing. To satisfy his wishes, Rembrandt's parents took their son out of school and placed him with a painter who was to teach him the basic rules of this art." It is interesting to note the author's casual remark, "to satisfy his wishes," made in reference to a fourteen-year-old boy. The novelty of such an attitude in Europe in 1620 becomes clear when one remembers that Molière, who was among the first to denounce rigid vocational training, was born in 1622. According to Jean-Nicolas Parival, a former professor of French in Leiden, such parental indulgence did not necessarily result in the children's disorderly conduct. On the contrary, in his work of 1678, *Les Délices de la Hollande* (The Delights of Holland), he says of misbehavior: *"Il est néanmoins surprenant qu'il n'y en ait pas encore davantage, et il n'y a peut-être pas de preuve plus assurée du bon naturel des habitants du pays et de l'excellence de leur tempérament"* ("Its surprising absence perhaps provides the best proof of the inhabitants' natural goodness and excellent dispositions").

Whatever the case might be, such upbringing soon created a firm understanding between parent and child, nourished by the former's forbearance and the latter's feeling of equality. The self-confidence felt by Dutch children probably made them conscious of their responsibilities earlier than children elsewhere. This aspect of Dutch education requires a word about religion.

Dutch religion was a family affair; the family was the source of all religious life, and parents exercised more authority as the natural leaders of the faith than as the more or less convincing administrators of parental severity. Religion conferred their authority with a legitimacy that needed no other confirmation. That the first religious feelings came from the mother, whose duty it was to teach her child to pray and begin its religious education, demonstrates the personal, simple form of devotion practiced in seventeenth-century Holland.

20. A Farmhouse amidst Trees, about 1641
Pen and bistre

Kupferstichkabinett, Dresden

Rembrandt confirmed the heart-felt nature of this religion, more dependent on compassion than on strength despite the teachings of Calvin, in every one of his great religious themes, particularly in the unorthodox *Repentance of Judas,* which he represented for the first time in 1629, and repeated several times thereafter.

The father presided at each meal like a ritual, saying the prayer with which it began and ended. According to Paul Zumthor, "No member of a bourgeois family would dream of being absent on these occasions without a very good reason." After supper, someone usually read the Bible aloud *(Fig. 3).*

21. Thatched Cottage, about 1640-41
    Pen and washes in bistre and India ink

    Albertina, Vienna

The First Emotions

One must picture the long evenings spent within thick walls against which the howling wind presses and swirls on all sides. Outside, the sky and sea appear threatening and wild, and one wonders how long the dikes will withstand the assault of the waves. Anyone who has not experienced a blustery night in Holland cannot imagine the bond that the wind suddenly creates and sustains across the country, passing among the inhabitants like a shiver, and from one house to another like a cry, to create a mysterious feeling that could be what one calls the communion of a nation.

His back aching with work, the effects of the night and of the wind, the young Rembrandt sits in the warm shadow beside the hearth and gazes at his mother who is bowed over the Holy Book, her face softly illuminated by the light reflected from the open page. To exorcise any spirits that might hover without, she reads aloud of miracles and fabulous characters. Little by little turbaned prophets and richly robed female sinners adorn the room while, as if by magic, the mother becomes dressed so ornately that when Rembrandt painted her in 1631 as he had seen her when he was a child, the painting was known as *The Prophetess Anna*, although the correct title is *Rembrandt's Mother Reading* (Earl of Pembroke, Wilton House).

The imaginary was commonplace for this unimaginative child. The Bible was as much a series of extraordinary adventures as a moral work in which the family tried to discover the hidden meaning or lesson. What was the significance of the story of Tobit? Why did Jesus chase the merchants from the Temple? What did the parable of the prodigal son teach? What was the purpose of Manoah's sacrifice? Each story contained a secret, which Rembrandt soon sensed to be the individual's ability to gain wisdom from every experience.

I cannot sufficiently emphasize the familial aura that surrounded the Bible and the simple, direct, everyday preparation of Rembrandt's world. If a certain Biblical theme reappears in his work more often than another, it is because, while he was a child sitting by the fire of an evening, his mother or father preferred to read a particular page by which they were especially touched or intrigued. For these modest souls the sacrosanct was modest; this is why they read and reread the Book of Tobit, enjoying the feeling of their similarities with the simplicity of Tobit and Anna. Rembrandt shows the life of this family in no fewer than five paintings executed between 1626 and 1650—an indication of his constant preoccupation with the subject.

By multiplying examples of this kind one could develop a theory of Biblical subjects in Rembrandt's works. The main themes exalt blind faith *(Tobit)*, participation in the Christian holy mysteries (I think here, notably, of the famous *Raising of the Cross* in Munich, in which Rembrandt mingles with the centurions) and, above all, compassion *(The Good Samaritan, The Return of the Prodigal Son, Christ in Gethsemane, The Denial of Christ,* and *The Repentance of Judas).* Is this not, in fact, an enumeration of the three theological virtues: faith, hope, and charity. Whatever the case might be, the family Bible became a personal affair for Rembrandt, and it was, significantly, the only book found in his home.

How can one ignore the relationship of such an analysis with the artist's early childhood? How can one fail to be impressed by the fact that all his life Rembrandt developed the conception he had formed of the world as he first saw it? Each milestone in the course of his life was predetermined within the family circle, and it is interesting to note that the major breaks usually pointed out in his life and work (1632, when he left Leiden to live in Amsterdam, and 1642 when he completed *The Night Watch)* correspond to more intimate ruptures. The reconstruction of Rembrandt's inner life, beginning with the loss first of his father and then of his mother, both represented by him so many times, will help understand the major divisions in his life and will explain the continuation of a childhood naïveté and spontaneity well into the artist's mature years. Saskia, the artist's beloved first wife, died in 1642, and Rembrandt's biographers usually attribute the enormous change in his sensibility to this death. However, I am inclined to think that Rembrandt felt her loss as a prolongation, and somehow the result, of his mother's death in that Saskia and the happiness she represented were contemporaneous with his mother. In this respect, I see in the little spectral face of a child, with the features of an old woman, which appears in the center of *The Night Watch,* the portrait of his mother and of Saskia, united in death.

But we are ahead of our story. For the time being, Rembrandt is a child, illuminated by the noble deeds recorded in the Bible, who lets himself drift toward the blazing suns within himself. At the beginning of this endless trip into the infinite, Rembrandt recalls Frédéric Moreau in Flaubert's *L'Éducation Sentimentale,* and we might say that *"Il ne voyagea pas, il ne connut pas la mélancolie des paquebots, les froids réveils sous la tente, l'étourdissement des paysages et des ruines, l'amertume des sympathies interrompues. Il ne revint pas, parce qu'il n'était pas parti ..."* ("He did not travel, he knew not the gloom of steamers, the cold awakenings under a tent, the giddiness of landscapes and ruins, the bitterness of interrupted attractions. He did not return because he never left...").

22. The Annunciation to the Shepherds, about 1640-42
Pen and bistre, wash, white gouache

Graphische Sammlung, Munich

The Years of Apprenticeship

So, in 1620, at the age of fourteen, "to satisfy his wishes" Rembrandt dropped out of the first year of university to become the apprentice of a local painter, Jacob Isaacsz van Swanenburgh, who taught him the elementary principles of painting and drawing. Otto Benesch believes that Jacob was responsible for introducing his pupil to the work of Jacques Callot, whose influence constantly reappears in Rembrandt's drawings and etchings of beggars and street types.

Rembrandt owed his real formation as a painter, however, to Pieter Lastman, in whose Amsterdam studio he worked for six months. Together with a group of Dutch artists that included Jacob Pynas (credited by Arnold Houbraken as another of Rembrandt's instructors), Lastman had worked in Rome under the German master, Adam Elsheimer. He and Pynas returned from Italy enthused with Elsheimer's admiration for Caravaggio's realism and mastery of light. They had also learned from the great German master the importance of small-size paintings, so much in demand among collectors.

At the age of twenty Rembrandt returned to Leiden and, after opening a studio in association with Jan Lievens, began his career as an independent painter. His first endeavors date from this period. *Tobit and Anna* (Bentinck Collection, Paris) dated 1626, in which the admirably wrinkled faces and artfully patched clothes are executed in the manner of Caravaggio, and two years later, *The Presentation in the Temple* (Kunsthalle, Hamburg), are equally good exercises. The paintings and etchings of this early period are touching in their apparent homage to those who had inspired Rembrandt: Caravaggio, Elsheimer, Lastman, Pynas, and still others. But these influences must be noted quickly, since, within two or three years Rembrandt was to assimilate completely the lessons he had received.

Toward 1629, at the age of twenty-three, Rembrandt produced the *Christ at Emmaus* (Jacquemart-André Museum, Paris). Although most of the scene is shrouded in gray and brown shadow, a candle lights the figure of Christ, who is seated with His back to the wall. This is far removed from the conventional treatment of light and shade by Caravaggio's disciples in Utrecht. By placing Christ in front of the candle like a screen, Rembrandt created around His silhouette a mysterious radiation of supernatural light that terrorizes one of the disciples and causes the other to throw himself at Christ's feet. The rapid style and free conception of this great painting are those of an incomparable draftsman.

When one talks of Rembrandt the painter, one tends to forget how much the painter owes to Rembrandt the draftsman. As Claude Roger-Marx so rightly remarks in *Rembrandt, "Peindre, c'est dessiner encore"*

23. The Good Samaritan Arriving at the Inn, about 1641-43
Pen and bistre, wash, some corrections with white

British Museum, London

("To paint is still to draw").   In contrast to many great artists, Rembrandt considered drawing not simply as the preparation for a painting, but as a work of art in its own right, a means of expression as complete as etching or painting.   The study of Rembrandt's drawings in their chronological order (insofar as it can be established with certitude) reveals such a masterful graphic style and so imaginative a talent, even in the earliest ones, that chronology becomes unimportant. Roger-Marx has written, *"Dès ses débuts, la sanguine, la pierre, puis le roseau ou les pinceaux humectés d'encre noire, de bistre ou de brou de noix, sont parvenus à définir avec une telle fulgurance les matières les plus diverses, le pesant ou l'impalpable, le relief ou les transparences, ce qui dure ou ce qui passe, un choix si instantané a été opéré entre l'essentiel et l'inutile, qu'on peut dire de maintes œuvres de jeunesse qu'elles obéissent déjà moins au commandement de la volonté qu'à une puissance bien plus lucide encore"* ("From the very beginning, red and black chalk, then reed pen or brush with black ink, bistre, or walnut stain were effectively used to define the most diverse materials—weighty or intangible, opaque or transparent, durable or transient—and the essential was singled out so unhesitatingly that many early works seem to stem from a strength far more lucid than a simple act of will").

In addition to the influence of Rembrandt's drawings on his paintings, another element contributed to the extraordinary evolution of his art between 1626 and 1630. It was described at that time by the poet Constantyn Huygens when he came to visit the workshop of Rembrandt and Lievens in Leiden: "They no more enjoy the relaxations of youth than if they were satiated old men. ... How often have I wished these talented young men could moderate their indefatigable fervor out of respect for their frail bodies, which they abuse with this sedentary life."

Huygens' impression was caused by Rembrandt's zeal and love for his work, together with his ambition, although even as a young man the painter had directed his ambitions toward inner success rather than outward appearances. During these years in Leiden, Rembrandt was very much as he appears in the Mauritshuis *Self-portrait* of 1629 and in the British Museum drawing *(Fig. 2)*: the large, clear, introspective eyes which miss nothing; a sensual mouth that would seem made only for pleasure were it not rectified by an obstinate chin; wild, tousled curls apparently inspired by the fancies hidden beneath the forehead; and already the vivid dichotomy in *chiaroscuro* of the acknowledged (admissable?) and the secret (hidden?).

If the powerful, organic division of Rembrandt's nature is the key to the mystery he represents for us, then his incontestable mastery of the art of *chiaroscuro* becomes, above all, the expression of a split personality which he was able to dominate and overcome with incessant, frenzied work. The man Huygens saw in Leiden was on the verge of a long struggle with himself—a struggle made meaningful by an enduring fidelity to the first impressions of childhood, and lasting at least until 1640, when his mother died. Because Rembrandt found himself through this struggle, he was able to create the essential, imperative work that was to prolong, as well as renew, all his art.

24. The Holy Family in Joseph's Workshop, about 1640-42
Pen and bistre, washes in bistre and India Ink

British Museum, London

25. The Good Samaritan:
The Wounded Man is Carried into the Inn,
about 1641-43
Pen and wash in bistre, white gouache

Boymans Museum, Rotterdam

The First Commission

Rembrandt retained some connections in Amsterdam from his days of apprenticeship with Lastman and Pynas, and important personalities, such as Huygens, came to Leiden to see him. The latter did not hesitate to compare *The Repentance of Judas* to "All that Ancient Antiquity and Italy had produced," and in his enthusiasm he added that "In this work, the beardless son of a Batavian miller has outdone Protogenes, Apeles, and Parrhasius." Arent van Buchel wrote with somewhat more reserve that "There is much to-do about a miller's son, but rather prematurely" (cited in Otto Benesch, *Rembrandt*).

The opinions of these contemporary critics soon reveal a sort of rage for Rembrandt's art that quality alone does not explain. The painter and art dealer Hendrick van Uylenburgh seems to have been in large part responsible for the popularity in Amsterdam of Rembrandt's work, and an important commission by the surgeons' guild, headed by Dr. Tulp, was to stimulate and strengthen the trend.

The originality of *The Anatomy Lesson of Dr. Nicolaes Tulp* (1632; Mauritshuis, The Hague) was twofold: first, such a commission would have been inconceivable in any country other than Holland, where trade guilds were omnipotent; second, the order was given to a young artist famous for his portraits and not, as he is now, for Biblical scenes. It must be remembered that Rembrandt's contemporaries valued and solicited him for reasons very different from those that elicit our admiration and respect. Seventeenth-century Holland loved qualities in Rembrandt that leave us largely indifferent today, and it is significant that his downfall came as soon as he began to stray from the public's general conception of the artist, a conception they were willing to pay for. *The Anatomy Lesson of Dr. Nicholaes Tulp* was certainly novel in comparison to *The Anatomy Lesson of Dr. W. van der Meer*, painted by Pieter van Mierevelt in 1617, which shows the professor and his students lined up behind the cadaver in a frontal presentation that allows each one to recognize himself. Rembrandt did not hesitate to make the cadaver itself, on which the light falls, the center of interest toward which all eyes are turned, nor to group the surgeons on the left and place Dr. Tulp to the right of center. Despite the dramatic effect, the painting's novelty was not too daring for the public, it did not really break any of the rules of middle-class realism. Ten years elapsed before the scandal, and in the meantime Rembrandt was to know fame.

26. The Return of the Prodigal Son, about 1642
Pen and wash in bistre, corrections with white gouache

Teyler Museum, Haarlem

27. David Taking Leave of Jonathan, about 1643-44
Pen and wash in bistre

Louvre, Paris

The Death of Harmen Gerritsz

To understand the effect of his father's death on Rembrandt, one need only see the portraits of Harmen Gerritsz to know to what extent his son worshipped him. Here the miller is shown as an officer (Art Institute, Chicago), there, wearing a gold chain across his chest and shoulders (Collection of Mrs. Oscar Ashcroft, London). These different costumes are thought to have been invented by the artist, and for those who believe in the importance of his family in Rembrandt's life, the rich clothes might betray his desire to endow his people with their just desert. After all, appearances counted in middle-class Holland!

Rembrandt's departure for Amsterdam in 1632 was the most obvious reaction to his father's death. The artist certainly underwent a profound change at this time, since his leave-taking of familiar landscapes and beloved faces coincided with his bereavement.

28. Jupiter with Philemon and Baucis,
about 1655
Reed pen and bistre

Kupferstichkabinett, Berlin

The Wild Years

Upon his arrival in Amsterdam, Rembrandt lived at the home of Hendrick van Uylenburgh; there he met Saskia, his host's cousin. To the young provincial, the girl represented everything he had hoped to find in the capital: social standing (she was the daughter of the late burgomaster of Leeuwarden, and belonged to one of the best families in Friesland); comfort, if not riches; and, not to be underestimated, a family tie with Van Uylenburgh the art dealer.

Is it presumptuous to attribute such calculations to the youth? Although Otto Benesch reminds us of the young Rembrandt's entry in the album of a German traveler: *"Ein frommer Mut Acht't Ehr vor Gut"* ("An upright mind holds honor above estate"), he adds that according to Houbraken, the mature man sought in his relationships with others *"niet eer, maar vrijheit"* ("not so much honor as freedom"). In this republic founded on trade, freedom had to be bought.

On June 8, 1633, Rembrandt became engaged to Saskia; the marriage was celebrated on June 22, 1634, after she came of age. The financial help and social standing brought by Saskia, together with the important commissions he began to receive, made this an exceptional period for Rembrandt. Through his friend Constantyn Huygens, secretary to the stadtholder, Prince Frederick Henry of Orange, he was asked to present the latter with two works, *The Raising of the Cross* and *The Descent from the Cross* (Pinakothek, Munich). Both paintings were received with such enthusiasm that a Passion cycle was ordered. Furthermore, his biographer Joachim von Sandrart reported that his house in Amsterdam was filled with "almost innumerable young people of good families, who came there for instruction. Each of these paid him annually 100 florins; and to this we must add the profit which he made out of the pictures and the engravings of these pupils of his —amounting to some 2,000 to 2,500 florins each—and his earnings from his own handiwork" (cited in Ludwig Goldscheider, *Rembrandt*). My insistence on Rembrandt's material success during the years immediately following his marriage to Saskia is relevant to the frenzied speculation that gripped Holland at this time and was carried to the absurd in the craze known as "tulipomania."

The fashion for tulips originated in France and quickly spread to the rest of Europe. However, "the sudden spread of a plant disease in Dutch gardens produced several strange changes in its corolla, and the horticulturists took advantage of the new craze to reap advantage from this plant disease by producing many curious varieties of tulips" (Zumthor). The inflation created by this situation is indescribable; people in every social and financial bracket began to cultivate tulips. By the winter of 1636 prices had gone wild; in Hoorn three tulip bulbs could buy a house. The movement assumed feverish proportions, and then, the

29. Canal in a City, about 1640-41   Black chalk   Albertina, Vienna

following spring, the bottom dropped out of the market. For Rembrandt, it was impossible to remain aloof from such fashions.

Laden with flowers, precious silks, and sumptuous jewelry, the paintings Rembrandt produced at this time reveal the general mood of the country and seem to reflect success rather than happiness, whether it be in *Saskia Smiling* (1633; Gemäldegalerie, Dresden), *Saskia with Hands Joined* (c. 1634; Gemäldegalerie, Kassel), *Saskia as Flora* (1634; Hermitage, Leningrad), or *Rembrandt and Saskia* (c. 1638; Gemäldegalerie, Dresden). In the last painting mentioned, much is revealed about the couple's relationship at this time. The contrast is between Rembrandt's display of almost vulgar gaiety, as he lifts his glass and turns from the waist toward invisible onlookers whom he invites to witness his success, and the serious far-away look on Saskia's face, which she barely turns in apparent indifference to the festivities.

Almost every year of the marriage was marked by sadness and discord. In 1635 Saskia gave birth to a son, who was christened Rumbartus on December 15 and died shortly thereafter. Rembrandt executed an admirable sketch of Saskia holding Rumbartus in her arms *(Fig. 7)*. In 1638 a girl, Cornelia, was born; she was baptized on July 22, and died one month later. The same year, Saskia's brothers and sisters sued Rembrandt for having squandered the assets his wife had inherited from her father. When the suit was dismissed, Rembrandt filed a countersuit to redress the accusations by arguing that "his wife and he were more than richly endowed." As could be expected, his case was also dismissed.

From Release to Freedom

Behind the triumphant appearances, what sorrow and how many setbacks were hidden. Fame and fortune go hand in hand and Rembrandt had made money, but as early as 1637 he began to have financial difficulties which, unfortunately, did not deter him from the irresponsible acquisition of a house in the Jewish quarter. The house cost 13,000 florins, one-quarter payable a year after the sale and the rest within five to six years. The artist was never able to free himself from the debts he contracted at this time. But such considerations are of minor importance when compared to the birth of a second daughter—again named Cornelia, perhaps in an effort to deny death or to reaffirm life—her death in August, and, in September, the death of Rembrandt's mother.

As already pointed out, the loss of his mother caused a profound change in Rembrandt. It marked the end of an era during which the artist was reassured, first by the presence of both parents, who had formed and shared his childhood, and then by the continued presence of his mother, who protected him from the full realization that he had become a man.

And yet, Rembrandt seems to have prefigured this inevitable truth in an astonishing portrait of his mother painted in about 1639 (Residenz Galerie, Czernin Collection, Salzburg). At first the half-closed eyes, the toothless mouth, and hands joined in prayer give the impression of a very old lady, but on closer observation one is overwhelmed by the tenderness that must have moved this triumphant Baroque artist to produce such a lucid, almost cruel, portrait of his own mother. It is the very substance of the face and hands—used, polished, and ageless—that is important here. They no longer represent flesh and blood but something—a pebble, a piece of wood, or a mound of clay—indelibly marked by the wear and tear of the world. The whole is completely removed from life or death, in tribute to love rather than in accordance with any aesthetic principle. Although he is one of those most aware of this feeling without which no art is possible, Claude Roger-Marx faltered before this portrait: *"Ce serait donc après plusieurs années du plus extraordinaire succès, plusieurs années après l'épanouissement qu'apporta à Rembrandt son mariage avec Saskia que le jeune peintre se serait penché le plus tendrement sur sa mère vieillie"* ("It could only be after several years of the most extraordinary success and growth encouraged by Rembrandt's marriage to Saskia that the young artist regarded his elderly mother with the most feeling").

The inner struggle, the slow, difficult progress of the soul within a body reveals the inconsistencies of this period between 1630 and 1640, from the death of the father to the death of the mother, from release to

30. The Bend of the Amstel, about 1649-50
Pen and wash in bistre

Louvre, Paris

freedom.   Amid the innumerable contrasts and contradictions of his painting, one seeks the real Rembrandt. Was it the artist who in 1636 painted *The Blinding of Samson* (Städelsches Kunstinstitut, Frankfurt) with Caravaggio's *terribilità* in mind?   Was it the late Gothic painter who represented the series of scenes of the Passion and sought to capture movement, the *"beweechgelichkheyt"* mentioned with satisfaction in one of his letters in reference to *The Resurrection*, and applied masterfully in *The Night Watch?*   Or was it simply the man who escaped time, and in 1639 portrayed his mother with disregard for the fashion of his era?

51

Rembrandt himself was to declare that "painting smells badly," and, because they were created to be shown and sold, his paintings of this period (with the exception of the portrait of his mother which is more of a drawing than a painting) fail to answer the questions aimed at defining the artist. Much more revealing are his drawings, the *"prières quotidiennes"* ("daily prayers") as Delacroix called them, in which he made a statement for himself only. Until about 1650, when painting, etching, and drawing became three means of a single expression for Rembrandt, both his reasons for painting and the personality that gradually developed in his paintings would remain impenetrable without constant reference to his drawings. During this early period the drawings revealed, and served as a kind of laboratory for, the artist's sensibility or fate.

Rembrandt soon played with the effects of light and shade in his drawings. This was no innovation; Mantegna, Lucas van Leyden, and Elsheimer, to name only a few preceding him, had used the light of a hidden lamp for dramatic effect; but Rembrandt quickly abandoned these mechanical methods for a contrast of wash and line that made the light spring from the very shadows. Claude Roger-Marx accurately remarks that *"A la lumière observée s'est substituée une lumière inventée"* ("An imaginary light took the place of observed light"). This was Rembrandt's great originality as a draftsman, or should it be called a necessity since every great artist uses a media, above all, to express himself? By expressing the immaterial with materials which he shaped in reference to the core of reality, rather than its surface, Rembrandt succeeded in rendering feelings that seemed to stem directly from the soul, in a manner that the realists were incapable of before him: the serenity of *The Women in a Doorway (Fig. 11)*, holy fear before a *Dying Boy (Fig. 9)*. The anecdotal sketch was gradually replaced by the artist's endless personal monologue in which he stated what was essential within himself.

Perhaps, because they express an inner vision even when the scene is familiar, the drawings always seem perfect from the first. Rembrandt sketched with rapid, unerring strokes, using a quill pen, reed pen, or pen and brush, and creating strongly contrasting drawings in which the luminous areas are brightened by the very depth of the blacks. On the other hand, a pen stroke is sometimes heightened by a blotch; the shadow of a shadow made by rubbing a drop of ink, diluted with water or saliva, onto the paper with a finger. The wash is darkened to accompany a broad line and produce a tragic effect as in *Rumbartus on His Death Bed (Fig. 10)*, or lightened next to more delicate linework to create an atmosphere of happiness as in *Saskia Carrying Rumbartus Downstairs (Fig. 7)*.

31. Clump of Trees, about 1651
Black chalk

British Museum, London

In summary, beyond the beautifully powerful pictures suggested by the early drawings is the first real expression of the artist's soul through increasingly mastered techniques.   The soul, saddled with a demanding body and bridled by a constricting environment, makes concession to both by painting, while secretly preparing the most tremendous upheaval.

32. The Interior of a Kitchen, about 1646
Pen and wash in bistre

Pushkin Museum, Moscow

33.
Study of a Trunk,
about 1648-50
Pen and bistre, wash

Bibliotèca Nazionale,
Turin

34. Lioness Eating a Bird, about 1641
Black chalk and wash in India ink

British Museum, London

35. Amersfoort Canal, about 1647-48
Pen and bistre, wash

Louvre, Paris

36. Susanna and the Elders, about 1641-44
Pen and bistre

Kupferstichkabinett, Dresden

37. Boy Playing a Flute, about 1646-47
Pen and bistre, washes in bistre and India ink

British Museum, London

38.
Study of a Male Nude
Standing, about 1646

Pen and bistre, wash,
heightened
with white gouache

British Museum,
London

39. View of Gelderland, about 1647-48
Pen, brush and wash in bistre

Private collection

0. St. Jerome Reading
an Italian Landscape,
about 1652
Reed pen and wash

Kunsthalle, Hamburg

41. Christ at Gethsemane, about 1652
    Pen and wash in bistre

    Kunsthalle, Hamburg

42. Old Man Seated with a Stick, about 1650
Pen and wash in bistre

Kupferstichkabinett, Dresden

43. A Farmhouse, about 1653
    Pen and wash in bistre

    British Museum, London

44.
Female Nude Seated before a Stove,
about 1654–56
Pen and wash in bistre

Boymans Museum, Rotterdam

45. The Lion by the Body of the Disobedient Prophet
    (1 Kings XIII : 24), about 1655-56
    Pen and wash in bistre

    Louvre, Paris

46. A Girl Sleeping (study after Hendrickje), about 1655-56
    Brush and bistre, wash

    British Museum, London

47. A Cottage among Trees, about 1650-51
Pen and bistre, wash

Metropolitan Museum, New York

48. Study for the Good Samaritan,
about 1648-49
Pen and wash in bistre

Boymans Museum, Rotterdam

49. Clump of Trees beside the Water, about 1654-55
Pen and wash in bistre

Louvre, Paris

The Personal Ordeals

Most lives are marked by a rhythm; Rembrandt's was no exception, and to divide it into ten-year periods would not be completely arbitrary. Such a division will facilitate our analysis of the artist's search for his soul. If the years between 1620 and 1630 are the years of apprenticeship, and those between 1630 and 1640 mark the death of his parents and his progress from release to freedom in his thirst for life, then the following ten years are those of his solitude—the bitter fruit of his freedom.

1640-1650: The birth of Titus in 1641 was the only happy event of this period; the boy was baptized on September 22, and grew to adulthood. *The Sacrifice of Manoah* (Gemäldegalerie, Dresden), a monumental composition in which the angel announces the birth of a son to Gideon's parents, was probably executed by Rembrandt as an act of thanksgiving.

On June 5, 1642, Saskia made her last will and testament; she died a few days later and was buried on June 19. Exhausted by her successive miscarriages, she had been ill for several months, and Rembrandt had drawn her as an invalid as early as 1639. Saskia left her entire fortune to Titus in trust to Rembrandt, who was entitled to enjoy the income during his lifetime provided he did not remarry. This arrangement perhaps indicates Saskia's jealousy of her husband, which might or might not have been justified.

Although Rembrandt had studied himself in self-portraits from the time he first held a brush, the situation in which he found himself after Saskia's death, solely responsible for a ten-month-old baby, perhaps provided him with the first opportunity to be totally alone with himself. With only a few exceptions, notably the admirable London *Self-portrait (Fig. 2)*, all the self-portraits until then had revealed a didactic conception of the human face as described by Félibien in his *Entretiens sur les plus excellents peintres anciens et modernes* (Essays on the Best Old and Modern Painters) and by Le Brun in his *Physiognomie* (Physiognomy), a short treatise on the characteristics of anger, fear, and other emotions. Until about 1640, Rembrandt's paintings of himself laughing, angry, surprised, and unposed demonstrate his interest in physiognomical studies. Then he discovered his own glance. After 1640, he no longer considered himself an object of curiosity, but a subject for inquiry. These later, silent self-questioning portraits are very different from the loud drinking pictures that preceded them. Between the self-portraits in Weimar (1643) and Leipzig (1650) the gaze deepens progressively until it seems to reflect the artist's very soul, and the features come to exist only in relation to the glance, as if they were its tangible result. Within ten years, Rembrandt evolved from the anecdotal, accidental style of Baroque art to a transcendental treatment of the present, which already denotes the purest classicism.

Ten years of profound change were needed to accomplish this interior development, this piercing of exterior appearances, this apparition of the soul. To cite one example: Rembrandt waited until 1641, the year Titus was born, to first etch his father's mill, perhaps suggesting a wish to bridge the generations. With Rembrandt it is always difficult to disassociate the reasons of the heart and of the head.

This is true of *The Night Watch*, a large collective portrait of a company of arquebusiers that was commissioned by their captain, Frans Banning Cocq, "Lord of Purmenlandt." The admirably vivacious composition, in which cool blues and greens are balanced by warm tones of ochre and honey, represents one of the supreme moments of genre painting. But this time Rembrandt had carried his audacity too far; the public was shocked and scandalized. The painting was received in sharp contrast to the general satisfaction with which the clients of Frans Hals greeted his *Officers of the St. George Company* (1639; Frans Hals Museum, Haarlem) in which the men were aligned in two rows, their poses varied only by the direction of their gazes. Rembrandt displeased his patrons, with the exception of Banning Cocq who defended him courageously, by actually catching the men (as called for in the commission) just as they received the order to march. They are shown in great disarray as they emerge into the sun from the shadow of one of the gates of Amsterdam. While some right the shafts and pikes they had lowered to pass under the vault, others appear surprised either by the light or by the orders they have just received. Behind the captain, whose purple sash is the only bright spot on a black uniform that contrasts with the lieutenant's dazzling yellow garb, the arquebusiers' disorder really gives the impression of a "watch," which dulling coats of varnish only subsequently qualified as "nightly," until the work's recent cleaning.

The scandal created by *The Night Watch* demonstrates the profound ambiguity of Rembrandt's relationship with his contemporaries. First, there was a financial problem, for, while each participant in a collective commission usually shared the painter's fee, many of the arquebusiers refused to pay their part either because they felt the pose in which they were shown was undignified or because they were partly hidden by a comrade. They saw no reason to pay good money for such unflattering portrayals. But beyond these personal considerations lay the real conflict—the Dutch conception of art at this time. Instead of the group portrait that had been ordered, Rembrandt had produced a painting. Once again he had substituted his interior vision for superficial appearances, otherwise how could the little girl with the old woman's face have existed? The necessity of this ghostly apparition was seriously questioned.

50. View of the Amstel, about 1648-50
Pen and wash in bistre

Rijksmuseum, Amsterdam

But this sort of question, together with many others, no longer interested Rembrandt. His contemporaries' lack of understanding, coupled with the deaths in his family, drove him into semireclusion. He by no means withdrew from the world, he simply ceased to live a worldly life. He was surrounded by friends whom he preferred to portray, and many of his students remained faithful, including the Dutchman, Carel Fabritius, and the Dane, Bernhardt Keil. His reputation as a teacher remained intact. As for the rest, despite the outcry over *The Night Watch*, Frederick Henry, the stadtholder, continued to patronize Rembrandt and in 1645 acquired two new paintings from him: a *Circumcision*, a copy of which is now in the Brunswick Museum since the original was lost, and an *Adoration of the Shepherds* (Pinakothek, Munich), for which the impressive price of 2,400 florins was paid.

The success of Rembrandt's *Christ Healing the Sick* (1642-1645), a magnificent etching known as the "Hundred Guilder Print," because of the fabulous sum paid for it at auction, attests to the apparent stability of the artist's fame. But by this time, Rembrandt was no longer interested in fame; of sole importance were the "events behind the mirror," as Cocteau would say, consecrated by each work.

Rembrandt's severest domestic difficulties occurred during this period. Unable to cope with his students, his work, and his son, he engaged Geertghe Dircx, the widow of a trumpet player, who produced total anarchy in the household. Although Geertghe took good care of Titus, she also decided to take the father in hand; she seems to have succeeded in winning Rembrandt's affections since he gave her jewelry, and she, in turn, mentioned him in her will. But she was an hysteric, and when she left Rembrandt in 1649 a series of unpleasant lawsuits was instigated which hurt the artist's reputation in Amsterdam. In 1656 Geertghe was finally confined to the Gouda Asylum by her own family.

During the years following Saskia's death, Rembrandt must have been the victim of constant recriminations and innumerable scenes of jealousy, especially after 1645 when the angelic Hendrickje Stoffels probably entered his service; the friction between these two totally different women must have been a nightmare. Unable to bear it, Rembrandt, who had always been a city man, buried himself more and more in the Dutch countryside, which gradually opened a silent world to him and within himself, as attested by the masterly etching *Three Trees*, executed in 1643.

Far from the intrigues, lies, and pretenses of man, Rembrandt began to feel a growing conviction that art was not a profession as he had believed until then, but an obligation, the only way of attaining a certain

51. Houses beside a Canal, about 1645
Black chalk

Kupferstichkabinett, Berlin

truth. Henceforth, the artist no longer simply painted, he painted himself—his innermost self. His art became a stubborn suffering. Why? And for whom?

Rembrandt suffered and became more stubborn. Even during Saskia's illness he had gotten into the habit of leaving the city, and the series of thatched cottages *(Figs. 15, 18-20)* date from between 1640 and 1642. He was to draw many more poor, old, potbellied thatched cottages and farmsteads discovered at a bend in the road. Like the fields he feverishly sketched, the houses are usually devoid of human figures; the stark landscapes and uninhabited houses seem to be part of a deserted world. Take, for example, the sketch of *Thatched Cottages under a Stormy Sky (Fig. 18)*: despite the banal subject, the drawing provokes a strong reaction because, like every one of these drawings, it signifies the artist's unlimited and blind confidence in the permanence of the earth.   Whether vibrating in the high-pitched disturbance of leaves swept by a storm's wind or in the low-pitched peacefulness of a thatched roof, the lasting quality that explains and justifies all is ever-present.   The same passion, fierce in its solitude, bursts forth sharp and shrill in the religious drawings such as the extraordinary *Entombment (Fig. 14)*, in which the rapid, cursory lines tear the paper and flash like lightning in a perfect ideogram of suffering.

Rembrandt suffered, but he persisted.   His perseverance was true to the tradition of the Batavians to whom Claudius Civilis showed the possibility of freedom even in a land as inhospitable as the future land of Holland then was.

One must imagine the artist as he appears in *Rembrandt Drawing at a Window*, an etching dated 1648, or in the 1657 *Self-portrait* (Bridgewaterhouse, Lord Ellesmere Collection, London).   Wearing a rather high, wide-brimmed hat, he is simply dressed in a tunic attached at the waist.   His face has become fleshy; the nose is large and could be imagined red and gross, but the lips are made thin by bitterness; the triple chin is one with the neck.   The tenseness of the lower part of the face contrasts with the forehead which simply looks worried, and the profundity of the questioning glance defies interrogation.

The look is always conscious of itself.   It is a look of suffering and the suffering that comes from looking. It is a hurt look that remembers an unhurt world.   In *Rembrandt Drawing Before a Window* (Edmond de Rothschild Collection, Louvre, Paris), the painter looks at himself looking out the window.   And, finally, the look is twofold because art can compensate for life's defects and create a second, deep, silent, inner life based on a few manifest truths that have been disguised by world appearance.

For Rembrandt there are two manifest truths: the deserted countryside that confirms the duration of earth and things—the only continuity in an otherwise transient world—and gives a specific meaning to the most everyday, immediate aspects of life; and the religious themes he treated throughout these trying years, which reaffirm, if need be, his natural compassion, tenderness, and goodwill: *The Annunciation to the Shepherds (Fig. 22), The Adoration of the Magi (Fig. 68), The Holy Family (Fig. 24), The Good Samaritan (Figs. 23, 25), The Return of the Prodigal Son (Fig. 26), Christ at Gethsemane (Fig. 41)*, and *The Entombment (Fig. 14)*.

I have called solitude the bitter fruit of freedom, and Rembrandt's drawings confirm my statement: either man is excluded from the landscapes or he undergoes a holy transformation.   Rembrandt avoided his contemporaries, except for a few friends, for some time.   However, with the help of his two tenets, he slowly shook off his despair and began to draw his first totally human figures such as the *Boy Playing a Flute (Fig. 37)* and the *Study of a Male Nude Standing (Fig. 38)*, whose nudity and fragility announce a different, if not another, world.

52. View of Gelderland, about 1647-48
Pen and wash in bistre and India ink

Rijksmuseum, Amsterdam

1650-1660: The Final Break

Hendrickje was first officially recorded in Rembrandt's life on October 1, 1649, when she was called to testify against "Titus's nurse." The artist's solitude had been ended by this ever-present, submissive, beloved woman. The illiterate servant-mistress: her high forehead was as smooth as a pebble, she had a plebeian nose, full mouth, golden silky skin, and big black eyes which bespoke her self-sacrifice and fidelity. According to Houbraken, she was "a little peasant from ... Ransdorp, in the district of Waterland."

Rembrandt, the widower of a patrician, not only dared show himself with this woman who bore him two children (the first baby was buried on August 16, 1652; the second, a girl also called Cornelia, was baptized in October, 1654) but also chose to seriously portray, with love and gratitude, her goodness and heartfelt proud generosity *(Figs. 46, 73)*. Thus he revealed the extent he had come to scorn the opinion of his contemporaries. It is easy to imagine how bitterly the Amsterdam middle class must have judged an artist who defied their dearest principle, respect for convention. No longer satisfied with offending good taste and custom with his art, as in the case of *The Night Watch*, he now also flouted all social decorum!

Convention, custom, conformity—so many frozen words that freeze the world. But he who challenges the established rules of a society makes himself vulnerable to attack. Rembrandt owed money, and his creditors became increasingly demanding of this man who no longer inspired their confidence. The artist's increasingly eccentric behavior seemed to provoke a general feeling that he no longer deserved the marks of his social success—the Breestraat house, for example, bought in 1639 and still in large part unpaid for. When, in 1653, the owner of the house began to show mounting impatience with his tenant, Rembrandt borrowed money from every imaginable source in order to hold out a little longer.

At this time Rembrandt still represented himself as he appears in the 1652 *Self-portrait* now in the Vienna Kunsthistorisches Museum; his willful face is presented full face, topped by a jauntily perched beret; his shoulders are broadly squared; and his hands are firmly planted on his hips in the self-confident stance of a fighter ready for action. In spite of this apparent assurance the inexorable machinery that was to ruin him had been set in motion.

53. Study of a Clump of Trees, about 1651
Black chalk

British Museum, London

In 1654, because Rembrandt continued to defy the accepted norm by living with his mistress in the Breestraat house, he and Hendrickje were called before the Consistory Court of the Calvinist Church to explain their notorious behavior. They failed to answer the summons. It would seem that by July of that year Rembrandt no longer belonged to the Reformed Church, since at that time Hendrickje alone received an order to appear before the Consistory Court. According to his biographers, this abdication from the Reformed Church would confirm Filippo Baldinucci's theory that Rembrandt had joined the Mennonite sect which rejected all authority and allowed the individual to interpret the Bible. However, the Mennonites descended from the Anabaptists and baptized only adults, while every birth in Rembrandt's family was followed almost immediately by a baptism. Hendrickje's appearance before the church judges resulted in her exclusion from Holy Communion and an admonition to repent her ways, something she could not do in view of Saskia's provision for Rembrandt to lose the income from her estate in the case of his remarriage.

Rembrandt put to good use the year of respite that followed this financial and religious warning. Of all the works he produced in 1655, from the *Ecce Homo* to *Joseph Accused by Potiphar's Wife*, one dominates and characterizes this period; it is *The Flayed Ox* (1655, Louvre, Paris), of which Pierre Gascar has said in *Les Chimères:* "*Avec* Le Bœuf *écorché de Rembrandt, le sang se met à circuler. Il y a là l'annonce d'une éternité éclatante et sans dieu, d'une éternité de métamorphoses. Dans la toile du peintre rutilante de viande étalée, elle introduit comme le bourdonnement d'une mouche d'or.*" ("Rembrandt's *Flayed Ox* stirs the spectator's blood. It heralds a brilliant, godless eternity of metamorphoses. It introduces something like the buzzing of a golden fly into the glistening display of meat.") By immortalizing this perishable flesh, Rembrandt confirmed a new and essential truth: since art could transform death into life, through art the artist could escape all constraints, whatever they might be. He was perhaps thinking of his own death or of his financial difficulties.

Rembrandt constantly borrowed on one side to reimburse the other, rapidly worsening his financial status. His inability to manage money matters without Saskia's help was compounded by a passion for collecting that was the basis for innumerable follies. On May 17, 1656, as a last resource, he declared the Breestraat house in the name of Titus with the Board of Guardians, arguing that his son had inherited it

54. Trees and a River at Dusk, about 1654–55
Brush and bistre

Louvre, Paris

from Saskia. The transaction alarmed his creditors; when he realized his total inability to satisfy their increasingly insistent demands he asked the Town Council for the privilege of *cessio bonorum*—an honorable declaration of insolvency—which he justified by his "commercial losses and damages at sea." Although none of Rembrandt's biographers takes this excuse seriously, Descartes'description of the wild commercial enterprises in Amsterdam would explain the artist's last desperate effort to save himself, by speculating in spices. Furthermore, the town counselors who granted the *cessio* had no reason to do so on the basis of an untruth.

The insolvency court took over the affair and on July 25 and 26, 1656, it compiled an inventory of Rembrandt's possessions, which constitutes the most extraordinary existing document on the artist. It reveals a total absence of any physical comfort—kitchen utensils, linen, plates and dishes, furniture—proving that despite his flashy success, Rembrandt had remained faithful to the frugality of his adolescence. In contrast, his collections contained the most beautiful, rarest, and most costly objects; they brought together and summarized the tastes and passions of a man, who, although he never left his country, maintained a roving and adventurous spirit to the end of his days.

The amazing humanity of Rembrandt's genius perhaps lay in the fact that no art was foreign to him. He was as interested in the art of antiquity as in that of the Far East; he owned works by the Italian masters, which undoubtedly explains why he did not feel compelled to make the traditional trip to Rome; and he owned works by contemporary artists for whom he was generous in his praise. He was also keenly interested in the natural sciences, and one can imagine his delight before the resplendent shiploads of fine materials and strange objects brought by the Dutch from the Far East.

Rembrandt's collection of Italian work included a portrait by Palma Vecchio *(The Rich Man); The Burning Camp* by Jacopo Bassano; a *Head* by Raphael; several copies "in the manner of Annibale Carracci"; a large painting of *The Good Samaritan* by Giorgione; and a *Child* by Michelangelo, together with portfolios containing "drawings by masters of the world," engravings by, or in the manner of, the Carracci, Guido Reni, and José Ribera, another container of "very large format, with almost all of Titian's works," and a "portfolio full of works by Michelangelo."

Old and contemporaneous Dutch and Flemish works equaled those of the Italians in quality and quantity: a great many pieces by Adriaen Brouwer; drawings and paintings by Jan Lievens, the friend with whom Rembrandt had opened a studio at the beginning of his career; Pieter Lastman; Jan Pynas; the marine

84

55. View over Het IJ with Sailboats Anchored at Port, about 1652
Black chalk

Albertina, Vienna

painters Jan Porcellis and Simon de Vlieger; Govaert Jansz; Hercules Seghers; Lucas van Leyden; Dirck Hals; Aertgen van Leiden; Grimmer; and Abraham Vinck.

A brief enumeration of the graphic art that made up the richest part of the collection follows. The Flemish and Dutch were represented by engravings and woodcuts by Lucas van Leyden, work by Bruegel the Elder, Goltzius, Maerten van Heemskerck (the entire work), Frans Floris, Abraham Bloemaert, Jan Lievens, Ferdinand-Bol, and Jan Joris van Vliet after works by Rembrandt. Flemish: Jordaens, Anthony van Dyck, Rubens. German: Martin Schongauer, Lucas Cranach, Hans Holbein, Albrecht Dürer, and others. Italians: "The valuable work of Mantegna," and engravings by, or after, Vani, Barocci, Raphael, Michelangelo, Il Rosso the Carracci, and others. French: Jacques Callot.

The list of objects reveals a taste for rarity as well as refinement: a strange animal, a beautiful cloth, Chinese and Japanese lacquers, porcelains, bronzes, an iron shield ornamented with figures by Metzys, inlaid weapons and objects in copper, pewter, and marble. To these must be added "forty-seven land and sea specimens of natural history, twenty-three terrestrial or marine animals, and a great many shells, sea plants, plaster casts made after nature and other curiosities."

It took three public auctions to dispose of the objects alone: weapons, sculptures, musical instruments, breastplates, shields, helmets. The first was in December, 1657, the second and third in February and September, 1658. The loss Rembrandt must have felt at the dispersal of treasures he had spent a lifetime collecting marked the final breakaway. The world had reclaimed everything it had given him.

But Rembrandt was a man of unlimited resources and, like the phoenix, of which he had made an allegorical etching, he was reborn from his own ashes. He overcame the despair of his dispossession to create his greatest masterpieces. Besides his best portraits, like the *Portrait of Jan Six* (1655; Six Collection, Amsterdam, *Fig. 62*), the *Portrait of Hendrickje Stoffels as Flora* (c. 1653; Metropolitan Museum, New York), and *Bathsheba*

56. Christ in the Storm on the Sea of Galilee
Pen and bistre

Kupferstichkabinett, Dresden

(1654; Louvre, Paris), he also painted *The Anatomy Lesson* commissioned by Dr. Joan Deijman's students (1656; Rijksmuseum, Amsterdam). The frontal representation of the foreshortened cadaver in this last work bears a striking resemblance to the body in Mantegna's *Dead Christ* (Brera, Milan).

From year to year, Rembrandt's paintings, like his personality, became increasingly stark; they tended to consist only of a light around which the scene or face was composed. *Jacob Blessing the Sons of Joseph* (1656; Gemäldegalerie, Kassel) or the *Denial of St. Peter* (1660; Rijksmuseum, Amsterdam) exemplify this use of light that vibrates with life and "congeals" into something that can be modeled. Between 1657 and 1660, when matters were at their worst for Rembrandt, he questioned himself, observed himself, looked at himself, and produced—in a burst of light—a series of self-portraits that are interesting, above all, for their different glances in which the soul appears and justifies all.

Rembrandt had come a long way from the time when it was possible to distinguish the painter from the inner man; the two had fused to become a single certainty of the appeasing quality of art despite the anguish it entails. This he expressed around 1657 in *David Playing the Harp before Saul* (Mauritshuis, The Hague). Art had become the complete expression of the man and, as the drawings of this period show, also his great consolation. In the walks he took through the countryside around Amsterdam, Rembrandt yielded to the pleasure of sight. His landscapes were no longer tragic, colored by his inner conflicts. In *A Cottage among Trees (Fig. 47)*, *View over Het IJ with Sailboats Anchored at Port (Fig. 55)*, *Clump of Trees beside the Water (Fig. 49)*, scenes of mills beside canals *(Figs. 71, 76)*, and perhaps the most accomplished drawing, *Trees and a River at Dusk (Fig. 54)*, the quiet, serene, motionless moments of the hazy dusk that precede the peace of night replace the tormented skies and trees agitated by stormy winds. During this period Rembrandt even drew his nudes with the same inner vision that dared to see the world as it is. Whereas in his youth the artist had painted nudes with cruel mercilessness, toward the end of his career the rebel learned to compromise, as we see in *Female Nude Seated before a Stove (Fig. 44)*, whose elbow partly hides the folds of her stomach and thighs, and in *Seated Female Nude (Fig. 63)*, whose pose gives the skin its luster.

As if to furnish additional proof of the serenity that came to him with resignation, Rembrandt executed an admirable *chiaroscuro* drawing of a family bustling around a slaughtered ox *(Fig. 66)* in answer to the earlier *Flayed Ox*. This drawing no longer represents a metamorphosis of death, but simply a scene from everyday life. It represents a time of simplicity for Rembrandt, a joyful time, above and beyond misfortune.

57. The Commiseration of Christ, about 1656
Pen and bistre, wash

Kobberstiksamling, Copenhagen

58. The Meeting of Jacob and Laban, about 1654-55
Pen and bistre, wash

Kobberstiksamling, Copenhagen

59. Study of a Female Nude
Standing by a Chair,
about 1661
Pen and wash in bistre

British Museum, London

60. The Baptism of the Eunuch, about 1655
   Reed pen and bistre

   Graphische Sammlung, Munich

61.
Young Girl Asleep,
about 1655-56

Pen and brush
in bistre

Kupferstichkabinett
Dresden

62. Portrait of Jan Six, about 1655
Pen and wash in bistre

Louvre, Paris

63. Seated Female Nude, about 1654-56
Pen and brush in bistre

Graphische Sammlung, Munich

64.
Portrait of a Syndic,
about 1662-65

Reed pen and bistre,
white gouache

Louvre, Paris

65. Lion Lying Down, about 1660-62
Pen, brush and wash in bistre

Boymans Museum, Rotterdam

The Last Years

Through a kind of intrinsic fate Rembrandt's last years, between 1660 and 1669, were like a dreadful duplication of his life up until then, and the misfortunes that mark this period blindly repeat his worst experiences.

Having lost Hendrickje (probably in 1662), Titus, his beloved son, and Magdalena van Loo, his daughter-in-law, in 1669, Rembrandt found himself as alone before his death, on October 4, 1669, as he had been when he lost Saskia—with the difference that, instead of one child, he was responsible for two, Cornelia, the daughter Hendrickje bore him and Titia, a granddaughter born after Titus's death. Also, he had been a wealthy man when Saskia died, whereas an old servant heard him complain at the end of his life that he had to use Cornelia's small savings to run the house.

The repetition and aggravation of this solitude is almost unimaginable. It is as though the elderly Rembrandt were once again called to account for himself. Upon closer analysis one sees that this last period provides numerous similarities with the past; comparisons grow and spread like wildfire, to make a final blaze in which the real significance of Rembrandt's life lies.

Opposed to the losses, trials, and solitude of the end were the last masterpieces. Châteaubriand said in *La Vie de Rancé*, "*Souvent les hommes de génie ont annoncé leur fin par des chefs-d'œuvre: c'est leur âme qui s'envole*" ("Often a genius announces his own end with the creation of a masterpiece: his soul has been released"). If one accepts the idea that every destiny is governed by its own logic, then the logic of Rembrandt's destiny was to prove life with art after he had striven so long to prove art with life.

The reversal had come full term. To prove life with art meant that art must henceforth give life its meaning, while until then life and its perils had given art its deepest significance. The change is in part explained by the contrast between the pains Rembrandt still took to represent himself as a resolute, decisive man in the 1658 *Self-portrait* (Frick Collection, New York) and the lack of all effort to please or impress in the *Self-portrait*, dated 1660, now in the Louvre. In the later painting only the truth of the gaze is important; Rembrandt placed himself before his easel with brushes and palette in hand to assert the essential necessity of painting despite the physical or social hardships endured. He chose to affirm himself in this manner at the moment that he at last dared to see himself without complacency; unimportant are the flaccid, drawn face, unshaven beard, and swollen red eyelids. The eyes have obviously ceased to be interested in the exterior world, and their tenacious expression could come only from some inner vision. It would seem that already

66. Flayed Ox, about 1655
Pen and wash in bistre

Kupferstichkabinett, Berlin

67. An Encampment by the Roadside, about 1654-55
Reed pen and bistre, wash

British Museum, London

68. The Adoration of the Magi, about 1657
Quill pen and bistre

Graphische Sammlung, Munich

in 1660 Rembrandt was no longer of this world.   In the words of Châteaubriand, *"La vieillesse est une voyageuse de nuit: la terre lui est cachée; elle ne découvre plus que le ciel"* ("Age is a night traveler who cannot see the earth and can only discover heaven").

Once again financial considerations had brought about circumstances that poisoned Rembrandt's life and made the inner vision so apparent in his last works.   In 1660 the loss of his civil liability had marked the nadir of his social status.   On December 15, Hendrickje and Titus had founded an association expressly to include Rembrandt as an employee in the painting, curio, and engraving trade they had managed for two years.   By this means, the painter was housed, fed, and protected from his creditors.   But one can imagine the disgrace he must have felt at this dependency on his family, especially within the materialist ambience of Calvinist Holland.

69. An Avenue of Trees, about 1654-55
Reed pen and wash in bistre

Kupferstichkabinett, Berlin

Things went very quickly from the moment art, to which Rembrandt had sacrificed so much, became his last resource and only justification; it was as if he felt obliged to prove that his art could justify the follies and misfortunes, the joys and deceptions. With each canvas he consecrated the tragic last years to the creation of a summary, or rather a repetition, of his whole work. Each one of these late paintings can be understood only, I believe, as an idealized "answer" to one of the early or mature paintings.

When Hendrickje first contracted the illness that was to prove fatal, Rembrandt received an official commission recalling the order for *The Night Watch* that he received when Saskia was dying. This time Govaert Flinck, a former student of Rembrandt's, had been asked to decorate the new Amsterdam Town Hall with illustrations of passages chosen by the poet Joost van den Vondel from Tacitus, to highlight the life of Julius Civilis, the national hero who led the Batavian rebellion against the Romans. After Flinck died

70. Daniel
in the Lions' Den,
about 1652

Reed pen and bistre,
wash,
some white gouache

Rijksmuseum,
Amsterdam

71. "Het Molentje," Seen from the Amsteldijk, about 1654-55
Pen and bistre, wash

Albertina, Vienna

in 1660 the decoration was divided between several artists; Rembrandt was to represent the Batavians gathered at night in the *Shakerbosch* around Julius Civilis, the conspirator.

When Rembrandt hung the finished painting in the Town Hall, the Town Council asked him to make some changes. He ignored the request, and for the first six months of 1662 *The Conspiracy of Julius Civilis* remained in place until the council returned it to the artist. When, at the end of the year, the situation remained unchanged, the painting was replaced with the work of another artist.

Rembrandt cut up the large, unwieldy canvas and kept only the central part in which the group of conspirators is represented (now in the National Museum, Stockholm). The solemnity of the occasion is emphasized

72. Female Nude Surrounded by Drapery,
about 1661
Pen, wash in bistre and ink

British Museum, London

73. Portrait of Hendrickje (?), about 1655-56

Reed pen and wash in blackish-brown bistre

British Museum, London

by the immensity of the vaulted room in which the meeting was held, together with the placement of the banquet table on a raised platform in the center of the composition. How can one fail to see in *The Conspiracy* an "answer" to *The Night Watch*, even if only in the movement, sought by the artist with such application twenty years before, and here simply suggested by the crossed swords.

The painting of 1661 and 1662, commissioned by the syndics of the drapers' guild, presents yet another "answer" in the form of a new group portrait that is comparable to the first and even to the second *Anatomy Lesson*. Both the *Portrait of Jan Six (Fig. 62)* and the preparatory sketch for one of the syndics *(Fig. 75)* demonstrate the mastery Rembrandt had achieved in executing portraits in which the faces alone created an atmosphere of attention and tension. He no longer organized the composition around a central interest; the movement of the painting came from within itself. In *The Syndics of the Drapers' Guild*, the artist painted the scene from below, producing an effect of elevation and upward movement. The syndics are seated at a table covered with a red and gold cloth which emphasizes their black robes and hats; the meeting has come to an end, one man has gathered up his gloves, another has started to stand, while the president seems to be finishing a statement with one hand extended in a persuasive gesture. These actions and the lateral, left to right movement added to the initial upward motion, gives the painting a feeling of intense life. The *Syndics* was the last commission Rembrandt completed; it is undoubtedly one of his most important paintings, in relation not only to his other group portraits but to all of Dutch painting, including Frans Hals' *Governors* and *The Lady-Governors of the Old Men's Alms House* (1664; Frans Hals Museum, Haarlem).

In his last works—*The Conspiracy, The Syndics, The Return of the Prodigal Son* (c. 1665), *The Jewish Bride* (c. 1666), or *The Family Portrait* (c. 1668)—Rembrandt accorded more and more importance to his subjects' faces, treating them no longer merely as a field for interesting expressions, but as reflections of the soul.

The man and woman in *The Jewish Bride* (Rijksmuseum, Amsterdam) have provoked much speculation. Whether they are Isaac and Rebecca, Jacob and Rachel, Tobias and Anna is unimportant since, dressed in oriental robes of warmly harmonious red and gold, they have transcended all human love. There is nothing erotic or even possessive in the way the man places his hand on his wife's breast. Once again, we are reminded of Châteaubriand: *"Lorsqu'on erre à travers les saintes et impérissables Écritures où manquent la mesure et le*

temps, on n'est frappé que du bruit de la chute de quelque chose qui tombe de l'éternité" ("Wandering through the imperishable leaves of the Holy Book in which neither time nor measure exist, one is struck only by the noise of something falling from eternity").

Because only that noise is audible in Rembrandt's last works, no Biblical reference is needed to make *The Family Portrait* (Herzog Anton-Ulrich Museum, Brunswick) one of his most religious paintings. Every human relationship transcended by love is expressed in this voluntarily unfinished painting which contains every technique; the faces were begun with a brush, then worked with the thumb and fingers, while the rest was scraped in with the knife. This example proves that a painting does not even have to be technically complete to be expressive. Before such freedom one questions the very definition of painting. As *The Jewish Bride* confirms a transcendence (in this case, of human love) which reoccurs in each one of the later paintings, so in this period Rembrandt increasingly confirmed a transcendence of art that prefigured Baudelaire's presentiment of *"splendeurs situées derrière le tombeau"* ("splendors beyond the tomb") *(L'Art Romantique)*.

Each one of these great paintings is at the same time a technical "answer" to an earlier work and the creation of a new sensibility in the nocturnal region in which Rembrandt then stood—the "active night" so dear to Saint John of the Cross. To describe Rembrandt's interior vision, Fromentin invented the word *"noctiluque"*—a penetration of his own somber mysteries.

Perhaps the most startling, frightening, and convincing "answer" of this period is the *Self-portrait* (c. 1663; Wallraf-Richartz Museum, Cologne), painted in reds and golds on a dark, charred background, reminiscent of Hercules Seghers, which makes Rembrandt's laugh leap from the canvas. This laugh is perhaps no longer the grimace of the early self-portraits—or, rather, by the reversal previously discussed, it might be called something beyond a laugh; burdened with long and painful experience, it rejoins the early grimaces. Rembrandt's last self-portrait answers for all the others. It is by no means a disappointed old man we see here; despite the expression that slashes his face like an open wound and makes one think of Hugo's Gwynplaine, who was condemned to laugh, there is a kindness in the glance that gives the laugh meaning and serenity. Rembrandt seems to have adopted the thoughts of his contemporary Jan Comenius, cited by Otto Benesch:

75.
A Syndic, about 1660
Pen and wash in bistre

Rijksmuseum,
Amsterdam

76. "Het Molentje," Seen from the Amsteldijk, about 1655
Pen and bistre, wash

Ashmolean Museum, Oxford

"But what will the admirers of human wisdom say to that?   They will surely scoff at the old fool who from the peak of honor comes down to the lowest depth of humiliation.   Let them laugh, if such is their pleasure. My heart too laughs for joy, having escaped the pathos of error.   I have found the haven, farewell to fate and fortune!''

Rembrandt was evidently ready for the end.   He had watched himself live through a series of profound changes during which he fulfilled his life with his art, to which he was able to give its true dimension.   He

77.
Young Man Holding a Flower,
about 1665-69
Pen and wash in bistre

Louvre, Paris

78. Female Nude, Asleep, about 1657–58
Pen and brush in bistre, wash

Rijksmuseum, Amsterdam

literally went beyond painting and restored its sacred nature as he restored virtue to mankind. Beginning with *The Night Watch*, and under the beneficial influence of his drawings, Rembrandt transformed what had been a privileged form of representation and a means of achieving social success, into the only manner of expressing himself and, by definition, of being.

All was achieved that was meant to be achieved. It is not surprising that at Rembrandt's death one painting remained unfinished; it is *The Presentation in the Temple* (Stockholm, National Museum), in which old Simeon begs God to let him go in peace, since he has seen the light of the world: "*Nunc dimittis servum tuum, Domine....*"

79. Lion Lying Down, about 1660-62
Reed pen and bistre

Rijksmuseum, Amsterdam

Chronological List of Drawings Reproduced

Between the Age of 21 and 35

about	1627-28	Self-portrait	London	Figure	2
	1629	The Baptism of the Eunuch	Munich		6
	1631	The Reading	Bayonne		3
	1635	Women in a Doorway	Private		11
	1636	Saskia Carrying Rumbartus Downstairs	New York		7
	1636	Dying Boy	Paris		9
	1637	Head of an Oriental in a Turban, with a Dead Bird of Paradise	Paris		5
	1637	Two Studies of a Bird of Paradise	Paris		8
	1638	Rumbartus on his Deathbed	Amsterdam		10
	1640	View of London, with Old St. Paul's	Berlin		16

Between the Age of 35 and 50

about	1640-41	Thatched Cottages with a Cart in Front	Paris	Figure	15
	1640-41	Three Thatched Cottages	Stockholm		19
	1640-41	Thatched Cottage	Vienna		21
	1640-41	The Entombment of Christ	Dresden		14
	1640-41	Canal in a City	Vienna		29
	1640-42	The Holy Family in Joseph's Workshop	London		24
	1640-42	The Annunciation to the Shepherds	Munich		22
	1640-42	The Good Samaritan at the Door of the Inn	Paris		13
	1640-42	The Holy Family in Joseph's Workshop	Paris		1
	1641	Lioness Eating a Bird	London		34
	1641	Thatched Cottages in Sunlight under a Stormy Sky	Vienna		18
	1641	A Farmhouse amidst Trees	Dresden		20
	1641-43	The Good Samaritan: the Wounded Man is Carried into the Inn	Rotterdam		25
	1641-43	The Good Samaritan Arriving at the Inn	London		23
	1641-44	Susanna and the Elders	Dresden		36
	1642	The Return of the Prodigal Son	Haarlem		26

Between the Age of 50 and 69

The chronology of Rembrandt's undated drawings is debatable. We have followed that of Otto Benesch in *The Drawings of Rembrandt* (6 vols., London, Phaidon, 1954-57).

80. Cottages beneath High Trees in Bright Sunlight, about 1657-58
Pen and brush in bistre, wash

Kupferstichkabinett, Berlin

RENFREW COUNTY LIBRARY